KYLE ROTE, JR.
American-born Soccer Star

Other books by the authors:

By Edward F. Dolan, Jr.:
AMNESTY: THE AMERICAN PUZZLE
BASIC FOOTBALL STRATEGY
THE COMPLETE BEGINNER'S GUIDE TO BOWLING
THE COMPLETE BEGINNER'S GUIDE TO ICE SKATING
THE COMPLETE BEGINNER'S GUIDE TO MAGIC
THE COMPLETE BEGINNER'S GUIDE TO MAKING AND
   FLYING KITES
LEGAL ACTION: A LAYMAN'S GUIDE
STARTING SOCCER: A HANDBOOK FOR BOYS AND GIRLS

By Richard B. Lyttle:
BASIC HOCKEY STRATEGY
BASIC VOLLEYBALL STRATEGY
THE COMPLETE BEGINNER'S GUIDE TO BACKPACKING
THE COMPLETE BEGINNER'S GUIDE TO BICYCLING
THE COMPLETE BEGINNER'S GUIDE TO PHYSICAL
   FITNESS
THE COMPLETE BEGINNER'S GUIDE TO SKIING
SOCCER FEVER

By Edward F. Dolan, Jr., and Richard B. Lyttle:
ARCHIE GRIFFIN
BOBBY CLARKE
DOROTHY HAMILL
FRED LYNN
JANET GUTHRIE
JIMMY YOUNG
MARTINA NAVRATILOVA
SCOTT MAY

KYLE ROTE, JR.

American-born Soccer Star

Edward F. Dolan, Jr.
and
Richard B. Lyttle

DOUBLEDAY & COMPANY, INC.
Garden City, New York

ISBN 0-385-14098-3
Library of Congress Catalog Card Number 78–18561
Copyright © 1979 by Edward F. Dolan, Jr.,
and Richard B. Lyttle

PRINTED IN THE UNITED STATES OF AMERICA
ALL RIGHTS RESERVED
FIRST EDITION

CONTENTS

Chapter	1.	UNTRIED HERO	1
Chapter	2.	DAD WAS A GIANT	11
Chapter	3.	THE BLACK BANDITS	18
Chapter	4.	OPTION PLAY	26
Chapter	5.	A NAME TO REMEMBER	33
Chapter	6.	DRAFT PICK	40
Chapter	7.	ROOKIE YEAR	48
Chapter	8.	"SUPERSTARS"	57
Chapter	9.	ON THE RUN	65
Chapter	10.	WASHED UP?	73

KYLE ROTE, JR.
American-born Soccer Star

CHAPTER 1
UNTRIED HERO

The crowd of 19,324 fans shook rain-soaked Texas Stadium with a thundering cheer. It was so loud that it made you think the huge stadium was full.

It wasn't. But this crowd made you forget the rows upon rows of empty seats. This was a soccer crowd. It had spirit. Plenty of spirit. And this afternoon, even before the game started, the fans were ready to explode.

There were good reasons for the excitement. For one thing, the game between the Toronto Metros and the hometown Dallas Tornado would open the 1973 season for the North American Soccer League. And even more exciting was that it would mark the appearance of a local hero in the line-up.

He wore number 12 on his red-and-white jersey. He was a husky blond, 180 pounds of bone and hard muscle. He had an open, boyish face that made it hard to believe he was really 22 years old. And he wore a toothy grin that made it even harder to believe he might be nervous.

But nervous he was. Yes indeed!

Kyle Rote, Jr., had a famous name. And he was already a hero to many of the fans because of his starring play in college. But he was really an untried hero. This game was to be the first professional soccer match of his life.

The fans didn't help. Their cheering just added to all the pressure.

The thundering roar that erupted when the stadium announcer introduced Kyle made him sick with tension. But he ran to the center of the field to take his place with his teammates. He shook their hands and was even able to wave to the crowd. The cheering continued.

And there was a new explosion of cheers and applause when the announcer introduced Ron Newman, the Dallas coach. Every fan knew that it was Newman who made the big decision to put Kyle in the starting line-up.

Actually, it was more than a decision. It was a tremendous gamble.

Newman was an Englishman. Most of his players came from Great Britain or other foreign countries where soccer was king, countries where youngsters began kicking a ball when they were four or five years old.

Kyle, a native of Dallas, had not started playing soccer until he was sixteen.

Newman was gambling. But the coach knew that, if soccer was to gain a following in the United States, it must have American players. And he knew something else. He knew that Kyle had the makings of a great player.

True, Kyle might not have the polish of a foreigner. He might not know all the fine points of tactics. He might make serious mistakes. But there were other things that helped Newman overlook these faults.

Kyle was strong, a superb athlete. He always kept himself in top condition. He was smart. He was eager to learn. And he had all the desire a coach could ever hope for in a player.

But there was one other thing about Kyle that Newman could not easily name. He couldn't call it leadership. Kyle lacked the experience for that. But it seemed that whenever Kyle was on the field, everyone tried harder. Newman had seen it happen during practice drills and in team scrimmages.

Kyle gave his best and he brought out the best in others. At least, that's what happened in practice. Now, would it work in a real game? Newman was ready to gamble and find out.

Much was at stake for Kyle. He knew that he might not have another chance for a long time. In fact, if he let Newman and his teammates down badly, another chance might *never* come.

As center forward or striker, Kyle would key the Dallas offense. If he could not break free from Toronto defenders, if he could not blast the ball with his head or a foot, the Dallas offense would crumble. It was that simple. He could win or lose the game.

When play began, the rain was still falling in curtains. It was tough for the players. They had to peer through the downpour to see the ball and follow the action. And the ball itself was so heavy with water that long passes were impossible. Even short passes went astray.

Kyle, however, was glad to be in action at last. Most of the tension was gone now, and early in the game he made a discovery. The wet, artificial playing surface of Texas Stadium gave him an advantage.

Instead of suffering a painful carpet burn with a fall, something that almost always happened to him on a dry carpet, Kyle found that he could dive and skid on the wet surface like a circus seal without harming himself at all. It made him more daring, ready to go all out.

For a time, however, he had no chance to put his discovery to work. The players on both sides could not adjust to the wet field and the wet ball. And so the play surged back and forth, with neither team able to mount a real attack.

But then Kyle and his teammates managed to work the ball to the corner with a series of quick, short passes. There, Dallas winger Mike Renshaw broke free. He was ready to kick a centering pass across the Toronto goal.

In front of the goal, Kyle tried to find some

open space, but he was closely flanked by two big defenders. Kyle backed away, hoping to confuse them. They stuck right with him. In the corner, Renshaw could wait no longer. He kicked the ball.

It came high and seemed to be heading for an easy save by the Toronto goalie. But it was spinning. Renshaw knew what a spin could do.

As if guided by some magic hand, the ball began to curve away from the goalie. It hooked right into the gap between the two men guarding Kyle.

Kyle dashed into the gap, his eyes glued on the ball. Then he stopped and waited. The ball was coming right to him. It looked like a perfect pass—head high and floating. But as Kyle watched tensely, the heavy ball began to die.

Could he reach it in time? Kyle dove forward, stretching out like an arrow. He was sailing full-length above the carpet when his head pounded hard into the ball.

Then he came down. He went sprawling and sliding on his stomach across the wet carpet. He thought his shot had missed, but the roar of the crowd was exploding in his ears. He looked up. There it was—the ball against the net.

Goal! Goal! A spectacular goal!

The fans went crazy. So did Kyle's teammates. He barely had time to jump to his feet before he was almost smothered by a heap of Dallas players. They were slapping his back, jumping up and down, and yelling their lungs out. Some tried to hug him. Others tried to lift him high.

Kyle finally broke free and ran happily up the field, both hands aloft. Volleys of cheers echoed and re-echoed from the low dark clouds. It was a great moment for Kyle and the Dallas Tornado.

But the game wasn't over—not yet. In the next minutes, Toronto fought back and then tied the score. The tie stood well into the second half.

The fans, tired and chilled, fell quiet for the first time that afternoon. It looked as if their team would have to start the season with a tie. That was hardly something you wanted to cheer about.

But Kyle was not willing to accept a tie.

Again and again, he drove deep to the Toronto goal. He did not get the ball often, but he did throw the Toronto defense out of balance.

Knowing by now what Kyle could do, the defenders surrounded him each time he neared the goal. This strategy finally backfired and gave Dallas the break it needed.

Once again, Kyle was running toward the goal, looking for a pass. Once again, the defense came out to cover him. The ball ripped in from wing. At that moment, a Toronto defender made a mistake because he was too eager to keep the ball from reaching Kyle. The player stopped the ball with a diving foot block, but then failed to clear it. The ball popped up right to the feet of John Collins, one of Kyle's teammates. Collins, unguarded with an open shot, wasted no time blasting the ball into the net.

Another goal!

Dallas had broken the tie. Before Toronto could get an offense moving, the whistle blew to end the game. Now the fans could cheer a victory. And cheer they did—for both the win and Kyle Rote, Jr.

He had scored one goal and was credited with an assist on another. He had sparked his team's offense. And he was named player of the game. What a start in pro soccer!

The cheering sounded great to Kyle now. The congratulations from his teammates and his coach sounded even better. Newman was smiling broadly. His gamble had paid off.

In the dressing room, a happy Kyle tried to answer a flood of questions from reporters.

Now that he was a real hero, how did it feel? Was he nervous before the game? When did he realize his header had scored the goal? Would he have made that big leap on a dry carpet? Was the defense tougher than expected?

Of course, other players were questioned about the game and about Kyle's performance. John Best, a veteran player from England, made the most surprising comment.

He said he felt sorry for Kyle. The young man would be under tremendous pressure from now on, Best explained, because the fans would be expecting a repeat performance each time he took the field. In short, Kyle had given himself a tough act to follow.

But Kyle did not look at it that way. Sure there would be bad days. Certainly he would not score a goal and an assist in every game. But that was okay. Kyle had a different way of measuring success. If he could play every game to the very best of his ability, he would be satisfied no matter what happened.

Of course, winning was important. But it was much more important to give everything you were able to give. It didn't matter whether you were playing a game, running a business, or trying to get ahead in a classroom.

That was how Kyle looked at things. It explained what he stood for. And it told a lot about the way he had been raised.

CHAPTER 2
DAD WAS A GIANT

Although born on Christmas Day 1950, in Dallas, Texas, the first home Kyle could remember was the Concourse Plaza Hotel in the Bronx.

His early childhood was a little unusual. He used to play on the sidewalk in front of the hotel, and he long remembered watching the people hurry by. He wondered where they were going and why they were in such a big hurry.

He spent hours watching the people, but this didn't mean he turned into a shy youngster. Far from it. One of his earliest memories was of selling his dad's autograph to passing

New Yorkers for ten cents each. Kyle needed the money to buy candy bars. Of course, Dad put a stop to that as soon as he found out about it.

Kyle Rote, Sr., was a hero in the big city. He was a star running back with the New York Giants. Yes, Dad was a Giant. He came to professional ball after winning All-American honors as a speedy tailback for Southern Methodist University in Dallas.

During his first seasons with the pros, he and his wife, Betty, established their growing family in the hotel in order to be close to the team. In addition to Kyle, Jr., there were eventually two other boys, Gary and Chris, and a girl, Elizabeth.

Young Kyle made friends easily, and he enjoyed his role as the son of a famous man. It was really fun at school. But soon after he finished the first grade, Kyle's parents moved to a suburban home in New Rochelle, several miles north of New York City.

By now, Kyle was much more interested in sports than in schoolwork. In fact, he didn't think he was a very good student. But his second-grade teacher changed his mind. She had Kyle check the daily attendance list. The list usually had errors in it. When Kyle began finding the errors, he also began finding confidence in himself. Several years passed before Kyle realized that the teacher had put those errors in the lists on purpose—to challenge Kyle to find them.

A high point of his early years came when Kyle met some of his father's coaches and teammates. These famous men would impress any youngster, but there was one man who made a particularly strong impression on Kyle.

He was the assistant coach for the Giants—Vince Lombardi. Young Kyle met Lombardi before the coach won fame with the Green Bay Packers and later with the Washington Redskins. But Lombardi already talked like a champion. Kyle was fascinated.

Unfortunately, most of today's fans think of the late coach in connection with one of his slogans: "Winning isn't everything. It's the only thing."

That does not tell the whole story about the man.

Lombardi once told Kyle that the thing that really counted was how much you put into the game. Even a poor player could be a winner if he gave the very best he had. And if everyone on the team gave his best, it would be a good day no matter what the scoreboard said.

At first, this puzzled Kyle. It almost sounded like an excuse for losing. But as Lombardi went on to fame with season after season of winning football, Kyle realized that the coach's idea worked. It explained how Lombardi found success, how he always brought out the best from his players.

Kyle adopted Lombardi's idea in his own view of everything, including sports.

Sports were important in Kyle's neighborhood. A game of some kind—stickball, baseball, football, or basketball—always seemed to be in progress. It was a happy, noisy neighborhood.

There was just one cause for unhappiness: Kyle never saw enough of his father.

As a young man, Kyle Rote, Sr., suffered a business loss that left him $35,000 in debt. He was determined to pay back every penny, but it meant long hours of hard work. When he was not playing football, he worked at other jobs. He went on lecture tours. He announced sports events on radio and television.

Instead of coming home at the end of each long working day, he stayed in the city during the week. This made family life so difficult that it finally brought an end to the Rotes' marriage.

This was tough for everyone in the family. It was particularly tough for Kyle's mother, but she was determined not to let divorce cause bitter feelings or turn life sour for her children.

Kyle had just finished his first year of high school when his mother took all the children back to her native Dallas to begin a new life. There, Betty Rote enrolled in Southern Methodist University and began studying for a special degree in speech therapy. Meanwhile, she worked hard to make sure that her children continued to lead normal, healthy lives.

Thanks to his mother's determination, Kyle remained on good terms with his father, calling on him frequently for advice, and often enjoying his companionship.

But just the same, the move to Dallas brought a big change. Kyle had to get ready to enter a new school. And he had to find new friends, but this did not take long.

One day, soon after the move, he took his football and headed for a local park. There was another boy there the same age as Kyle, and he had a football under his arm, too. His name was Henry Davis.

Henry and Kyle quickly became close friends. When classes began at Highland Park High School, the two went out for the same sports and played together on the same teams.

Both boys loved football. In fact, football had long been Kyle's favorite sport, and he had already decided that he would become a pro ball player just like his dad.

At Highland Park High, Kyle began to show the potential. His famous name, of course, attracted attention. But his own ability sparked interest. It was not long before college scouts were buzzing about the young Kyle Rote. He definitely had the markings of another star.

Kyle's future seemed settled. He would graduate from high school and go to college, probably one of the big ones, on a football scholarship. Then, after college, he would join the professional ranks.

Kyle Rote, Jr. *(Photo: Richard B. Lyttle)*

Kyle Rote, Sr., gathers in a touchdown pass for the New York Giants during a 31–7 victory over the Philadelphia Eagles in 1955. *(Wide World Photo)*

As a Sewanee Tiger, Kyle is already showing good heading form. In his three seasons at Sewanee he scored a total of fifty goals. *(Photo: courtesy University of the South)*

Sewanee's peaceful campus with stone buildings and well-kept gardens gave Kyle a big change of scene and a new outlook on the importance of college life. *(Photo: courtesy University of the South)*

With fellow students, Kyle waits on the sidelines for an intramural game to begin. Intramural sports have always been popular at Sewanee. *(Photo: Bill Willcox, courtesy University of the South)*

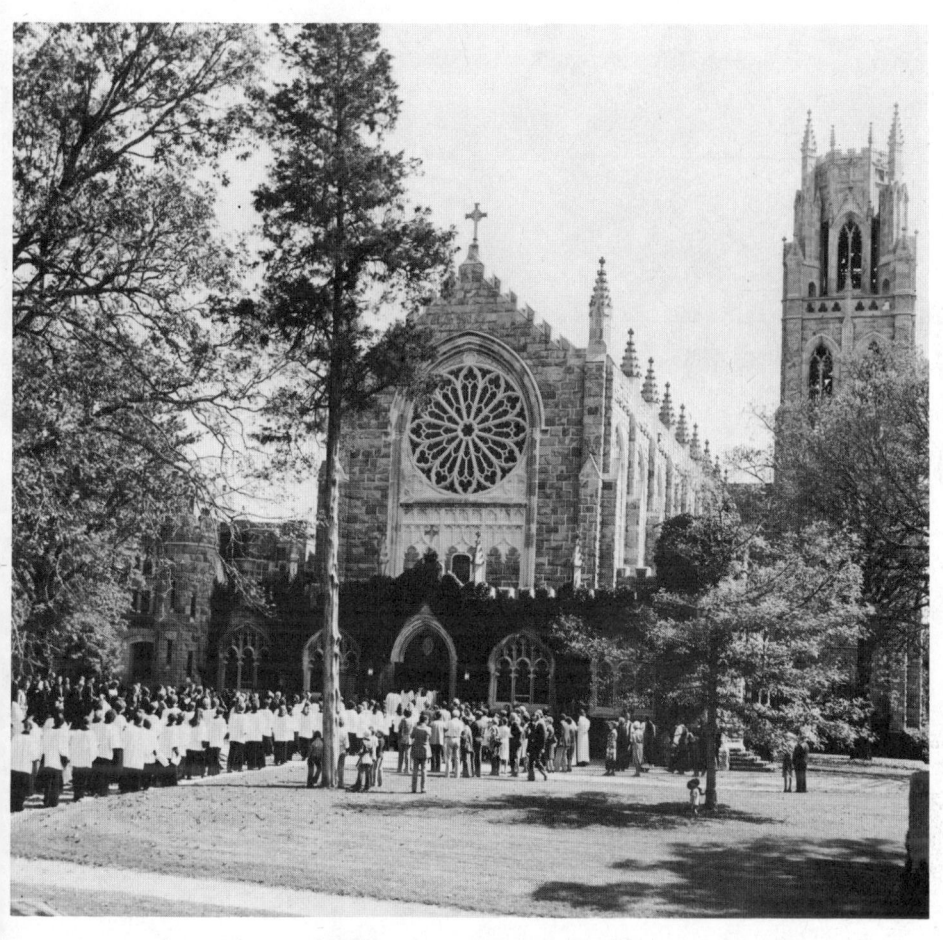

Looking like an old church in Europe, the chapel at Sewanee is actually a fairly new building. This photo was taken at the start of dedication ceremonies. *(Photo: courtesy University of the South)*

Kyle scores again and receives a teammate's warm congratulations as the fans cheer for their home town hero. *(Wide World Photo)*

League award winners pose for the camera after the 1973 season. Warren Archibald, right, was most valuable player. Philadelphia's Al Miller was coach of the year, and Kyle was rookie of the year. *(Photo: United Press International)*

Tension shows on the faces of Kyle and defenders while they await a referee's ruling at the net during a game with the Seattle Sounders. *(Wide World Photo)*

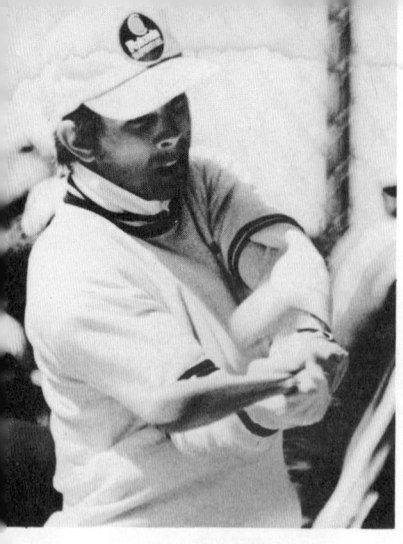

Kyle takes a mighty swing at the ball (just above wrists) during the batting competition of the 1974 Superstars. He failed, however, to win any points in this event. *(Photo: United Press International)*

Kyle gives a fan his autograph and a big smile after the 1974 Superstars victory. Broadcasts of the Superstars gave national television viewers their first look at Kyle. They liked what they saw. *(Photo: United Press International)*

After the 1974 Superstars awards ceremony, Kyle Rote, Sr., shows off his son's medal to admiring fans. *(Photo: United Press International)*

No one who saw Kyle play in high school doubted this future. Kyle himself certainly had no doubts. It was just what he wanted. At least it was at the time. He had no idea how much things could change.

CHAPTER 3
THE BLACK BANDITS

Kyle lettered in football, basketball, and baseball at Highland Park. Naturally, he had to keep himself in shape, but during summer vacations it was too easy to lose top conditioning with a few weeks of idleness.

So in the summer of 1967, after his junior year, Kyle, along with Henry Davis and other friends from the football squad, decided to try to stay in shape with some kind of summer activity.

But what could they do that did not need a lot of expensive equipment and a lot of supervision?

Someone mentioned soccer. United Dundee,

an excellent team from Scotland, was in Dallas at the time, playing exhibition games. A few of Kyle's friends went to see a game just to find out what soccer was all about.

They came back full of enthusiasm. Soccer would not only keep you in shape, they said, but it also looked like a lot of fun.

So Kyle and his friends made the decision that was to shape Kyle's future. They found some books, studied the rules, and began playing soccer. Soon after they had their team organized, they sent out challengers to all comers. And they began trying to think of a name for themselves.

It had to be a scary name, one that would command respect from opponents. No one in the group was black, but they all admired many of the black athletes. And there was a reckless group of football players at Louisiana State University at the time who called themselves the Chinese Bandits.

Why not call themselves the Black Bandits?

The name caught on, and it seemed to work. At least, the Bandits managed to beat most of the teams that accepted their challenge. Their success was surprising. They had very little skill. They knew the game only from what they had read in books. And for a while they received no coaching at all.

But then one day during practice, the Bandits were startled by the voice of an excited Englishman. He hurried onto the field, calling out to the players, telling them they were doing everything wrong.

Naturally, the Bandits did not like this, not right away. But soon, the things the man told them began to make sense. He seemed to want to help. And he certainly seemed to know the game.

Indeed he did. The man's name was Ron Griffith. He had come from Blackpool, England, to send reports back to British newspapers on United Dundee's games. He was a sportswriter who specialized in soccer.

Griffith explained that he was passing the playground in his car when he saw the boys playing—or trying to play—his game. He hoped they didn't mind, but he just had to stop and help.

He spent an hour with the Bandits that first day. He taught them to kick the ball with their insteps instead of their toes. He returned the next day for a longer session on the basic skills.

Soon, Griffith was working with the team just about every day. Before long the players began to improve. Then the unofficial coach started teaching soccer tactics.

Griffith, who was to settle in the Dallas-Fort Worth area and become a school soccer coach, began working with other teams. He wanted to encourage the growth of the game.

The summer after he discovered the Bandits, Griffith arranged a five-week tour of England for members of the Longhorn Soccer Club. Kyle was one of those who made the trip.

He was impressed. English soccer was a tough, fast game, and the trip opened Kyle's eyes to the international popularity of the sport. It seemed that soccer was big everywhere except in the United States.

The trip also made Kyle appreciate the mental side of the game. With the continual action of soccer, every player on the field had to be thinking ahead, planning his moves, figuring out what his teammates were doing, trying to guess how the opposition would react.

It was a challenge, and Kyle loved challenges—the tougher the better.

Thanks in large part to Griffith, the Bandits developed an enduring spirit right from the start. They are still playing today, and although Kyle no longer plays with them, he still finds time to visit with the players whenever he can.

But soccer did nothing to weaken Kyle's interest in football. No way!

When he returned to the Highland Park gridiron after that first summer of soccer, Kyle played quarterback and safety so well that he earned All-American honors. He also continued to play basketball and baseball. He did well in these sports, too. In fact, in his senior year, he was elected captain of both the basketball and the baseball teams.

But football remained his first love. And he certainly seemed to be on the right track. Long before graduation day, the scholarship offers began pouring in. Eventually more than fifty colleges were trying to tempt him.

This was not surprising. Kyle's All-American

honors alone were enough to spark national interest. In addition, he could run 40 yards in 4.7 seconds. Any college in the country could use that speed.

But some schools were too eager for Kyle. One offered him additional money as pay for a night-watchman job in the athletic dorm. All Kyle had to do was to be in the dorm from midnight to dawn. Kyle wondered when he would sleep. He could sleep on the job, he was told. All he had to do was be in the dorm.

Kyle knew that was an illegal offer and he turned it down.

He refused several other offers because he suspected that the schools put far too much emphasis on sports and not enough on classes. Sure, he wanted college to prepare him for a professional career in sports, but he also wanted an education.

For a time, Kyle was strongly tempted by Southern Methodist University, his father's and mother's school. Certainly, most of his friends and members of his family expected him to follow in his father's footsteps and lead the SMU Mustangs to another string of victorious seasons.

But that was just the trouble. He wasn't sure he wanted to follow in his father's footsteps. It bothered Kyle to think that everyone would constantly be comparing him with his father.

And there was a touch of the rebel in Kyle. Why do something simply because it was expected of you?

In the end, he chose Oklahoma State University. It was a football powerhouse, and there seemed to be a real interest at Stillwater in educating the athletes.

With the decision behind him, Kyle could relax. Now he could give full attention to finishing high school. It was good to think that his future was settled. He could see just one flaw in going to Oklahoma State: His friend Henry Davis would not be there.

Henry had decided to go to the University of the South at Sewanee, Tennessee. Kyle had already heard a great deal about Sewanee from his chemistry teacher and basketball coach, Dr. E. A. Sigler. Dr. Sigler, who later became principal at Highland Park, had attended Sewanee. He thought it would be just right for Kyle.

But there was no use trying to persuade Kyle to go there. Sewanee was a small school with less than a thousand students. It did not offer big sports scholarships.

CHAPTER 4
OPTION PLAY

The State coach called the play again. He was running a hard drill because he had to sharpen the squad's offense for the next game, the fourth on the frosh schedule.

Quarterback Kyle Rote, Jr., looked up at the fading light in the Oklahoma sky. He would be late for his 6 P.M. English class, but this was not the time to think about studies. He must run the option play once more and try to make it work slick enough to please the coach. Then maybe they could all leave the field.

The snap came from center. Kyle took the ball and began running along the line. If his blockers opened a good hole, he could run on a keeper. If no hole appeared, he could lateral to one of his backs for a sweep play.

This was the option, but to make it work, Kyle had to time his move at just the right moment.

Suddenly, a big, inviting gap opened in the defensive line. It looked like a highway. In a split second, Kyle turned and charged into the hole, running full speed.

Crack!

Kyle didn't see what hit him. He didn't feel himself fall. All he felt was pain.

Later, he found out that it was one of his own teammates, diving for a block, who had accidentally crashed into him, hitting the side of his leg, right at the knee.

He was rushed to the hospital. X rays showed a break in his thigh bone just above the knee. Ligaments around the knee were also damaged. Surgery was needed.

The operation was a success, but Kyle would spend the rest of the season on the bench with his leg in a cast.

No injury can ever be called a good thing, but Kyle's leg healed well. And being sidelined gave him time to think. He realized that he faced an option play in his own life.

So far, Oklahoma State had not been everything that Kyle hoped it would be. He was having fun, finding many new friends. There were dates, parties, and bids to join fraternities. And Kyle enjoyed his classes.

But sports came first in the eyes of the school. There was no way to deny it. State was no different from all the other big football factories. Your performance on the field was far more important than your performance in the classroom. Kyle already had the feeling that no one really cared about his grades.

Sports at OSU seemed to be run like a business. All the athletes at the Stillwater campus lived in special quarters. They did not have much chance to meet other students. The whole setup was more like a training camp than a school.

Kyle began to wonder if any school prepared an athlete for professional football and, at the same time, gave him a good education. Perhaps it might happen if the athlete could make himself study. Kyle knew he was not that type of athlete. He needed challenge and direction from other students and professors. And he would not find that at OSU.

Kyle made no sudden decision. Oklahoma State, after all, had a number of good points. Already he had received sound training under excellent coaches. His teammates were among the best young athletes in the land.

And Kyle could not overlook his scholarship. He must think hard before giving that up.

Back in Dallas for Christmas vacation, Kyle began hearing about Sewanee. Henry Davis could not praise the place enough. Kyle knew that Henry's uncle was on the faculty there, and that might explain a lot of Henry's enthusiasm. Just the same, the place did sound good.

During the vacation, Kyle looked up Dr. Sigler at Highland High. They talked about Kyle's future. Dr. Sigler did not want to urge Kyle to give up a scholarship. That decision, he said, could be made by one man only, Kyle himself.

On Christmas Day, Kyle turned nineteen, but was he old enough to make a decision that could change his entire future?

Before the holidays ended, Kyle and Henry were in a serious auto accident. Kyle escaped with minor bruises, but Henry was so badly injured that recovery would require months. He would not be able to return to Sewanee until the following fall.

But the accident, bad as it was, brought the two friends even closer together. They knew now that they would be friends for life. Kyle thought it would be great if he and Henry could go to college together.

Just the same, Kyle returned to the Oklahoma State campus undecided about his options. He was still weighing the good against the bad at OSU.

Soon after classes started again, however, something really bad happened to Kyle.

Unknown to him, there were a few athletes in his dorm who were thieves. For some time, they had been stealing tape decks out of cars and selling them to local dealers. The ring of thieves included some of Kyle's teammates and "friends."

Kyle had always trusted people, but after a while he began to suspect that something was wrong. He told his coach about it and said the school should investigate before it became a case for the police.

Nothing was done. A week after talking to his coach, Kyle and a roommate were arrested by Stillwater police.

It happened because he and the roommate had borrowed a car to drive into town to buy hamburgers. The car was loaned to them by one of the thieves. It was a car that the police believed was being used in the thefts.

Of course, Kyle and his roommate were innocent, but the police held them for questioning for several hours. Finally, three of the real thieves were brought in. Instead of clearing Kyle, however, they said that he was their ringleader.

Kyle was stunned. Apparently, the thieves thought that by naming a star athlete like Kyle, the whole mess would be hushed up. It did not work that way.

The next day, the story hit the newspaper under a big headline: ROTE AND FOUR OTHERS QUESTIONED.

Kyle simply could not understand how people could act this way, particularly people he thought were friends. They had lied about him, hoping to save their skins.

Of course, when the facts came out, Kyle and his roommate were cleared completely. The newspaper printed a retraction. But the experience disheartened Kyle.

He tried not to let it influence his decision. And when spring practice came he worked hard so that no one could accuse him of letting himself or his teammates down.

But when the school year ended, Kyle knew that he would not return to Oklahoma State. Although it might ruin his hopes for a professional career in football, he would enroll in the University of the South at Sewanee.

CHAPTER 5
A NAME TO REMEMBER

The Black Bandits once again worked the ball upfield into Dallas Tornado territory. Once again, Kyle led the Bandit's attack. He passed off and ran for the Dallas goal, hoping for a return pass that would give him a clean shot.

But the return pass did not come. Kyle was guarded too closely by a Dallas defender. Kyle's teammates simply could not risk trying to kick the ball to him.

This was not a serious game—at least, not for the Dallas players and their coach. It was the summer of 1969, Ron Newman's second year as Tornado coach. He had called this scrimmage with the Bandits simply to give his players a good workout.

Of course, Newman always had an eye out for new talent, and he had heard about Rote. But so far, the husky blond had done nothing.

Sure, the lad looked big and strong. But he just did not seem able to move against a smart defense. It was too bad, Newman decided, but young Rote was just another, typical American soccer player—all desire and no skill. At least not enough skill to—

Then it happened!

Kyle's defender dropped a step behind during another run on goal. A pass came in. Wham! The ball almost ripped the back of the net. Goal for the Bandits!

While Kyle and his teammates celebrated, Newman just stared. This man Rote had just kicked one of the hardest shots Newman had ever seen.

Interesting? Yes indeed! But maybe it was just a lucky shot.

Newman paid close attention as play resumed. He watched the Bandits launch another offense. He saw Kyle running hard. And once again, he saw him outrun his defender.

And there was the pass again—the same play. Wham! Another whistling goal for the Bandits. Rote had done it again.

Newman was impressed. Here was a man to watch. Even in a tough English league, he might be a prospect. Yes, Kyle Rote, Jr., was a name to remember.

But while Newman remembered Kyle's performance against the Tornado, Kyle was too busy in the months that followed to give it much thought.

At Sewanee, Kyle hoped to play both soccer and football, but he found that this would not be possible because of conflicting schedules. He would have to make a choice. He decided on soccer.

Sportswriters who had been following Kyle's career were jolted when he went to Sewanee. Stories appeared in newspapers across the country to say that Kyle was giving up a sure spot in the defensive backfield for OSU, maybe even giving up a real chance to become the next quarterback for the Dallas Cowboys. Why? Because Kyle Rote, Jr., liked soccer more than football.

It was true. Even Kyle himself was surprised, but it was true. There was nothing wrong with football, Kyle told reporters. It was certainly the No. 1 sport in America. But soccer was growing. It would soon be a major sport.

"I want to be part of that growth," Kyle said.

Soccer was growing fast at Sewanee. The Tigers were just in their second varsity year when Kyle joined the team, but already they were gaining respect in the tough College Athletic Conference, where play was more competitive in soccer than it was in football.

In their first season, the Tigers posted a record of three wins, eight losses, and one tie. They improved on that greatly in their second year with six wins, five losses, and one tie. One reason for the improvement was Kyle. He led the Tiger offense with seventeen goals.

A good record, and many other good things were happening for Kyle at Sewanee.

For one thing, he was forced to buckle down and study. He began earning good grades. Much of this was because the professors were really interested in giving their students the best education possible. And since the college was small—just 991 students when Kyle enrolled—everyone in class got plenty of individual attention from the teachers.

Kyle discovered this when he signed up for Dr. Charles Peyser's course in psychology. The course was required, and Kyle was not too interested in it. But after Kyle scored a C on the first quiz, Dr. Peyser teamed him with a laboratory partner who was a straight-A student. The smart partner challenged Kyle and fired his competitive spirit. Kyle studied for hours, but it paid off. He scored A's in all of the tests that followed. He was on his way to honor-student ranks at Sewanee.

Later, Kyle and Dr. Peyser became good friends, and Kyle served as a teaching assistant in the doctor's lab.

The small-town feeling at Sewanee was perfect. Located near Tennessee's southern border, the town had just one movie house and one shopping center. It was surrounded by green hills and open meadows.

The campus itself was entirely different from Oklahoma State's big campus. Here there were no special dorms for athletes. Henry Davis, Kyle's roommate, was an athlete, but they were surrounded by students who could talk for hours about the theater, art, history, music, and many other things that interested Kyle.

Most of the social life centered around the fraternity houses where the students ate their meals. Kyle joined the Delta Tau Delta fraternity. He began leading them at once to victories in intramural sports.

The victories were due in part to Kyle's own talent. But he also had the ability to bring out the best from others on his team.

Kyle was soon elected treasurer of the Delts.

He was elected to many other important posts during his college career. He became a head proctor and served as vice president of the Order of Gownsmen, the students' governing body. He was a member of the discipline committee, the delegate assembly, the student forum, and the committee on standards and privileges. He was chairman of the elections committee. He was named sports editor and then associate editor of the *Sewanee Purple*, a school publication. He served as captain of the soccer team for two years, and captain of the track team for one year. In track, he could toss the javelin more than two hundred feet.

On top of all this, Kyle found time to coach soccer at a local high school for three years.

All these jobs took time and hard work. If Kyle had a major fault at Sewanee, it was taking on too much work. But it never seemed to bother him. He felt he had to do as much as he could. It was his responsibility. He explained it this way:

"From those to whom much is given, much is expected."

Kyle also knew that the more he gave, the more he would receive. And he was receiving much from Sewanee—a solid education, maturity, friendship and fun.

Long before his first year ended, Kyle knew he had made the right choice in coming to Sewanee. And this was before he fell in love.

CHAPTER 6
DRAFT PICK

She was a pretty blonde, and she was smart. Mary Lynne Lykins came to Sewanee from Roseville, Georgia, as a scholarship student. She was one of the first girls admitted after Sewanee went from being an all-male to a coed college.

She and Kyle had an unusual courtship. There was very little dating among the students. Kyle and Mary Lynne became friends in the classroom. Then they discovered that they enjoyed talking with each other after class and at various student gatherings.

One of the best times for a long talk came after evening chapel. The two didn't go

Close to the goal and between two San Jose defenders, Kyle slams down a header in a typical high-jumping attack. Both Dallas and San Jose showed lots of offense in this 1974 contest, but San Jose won, 4–3. *(Photo: Donald Echeverria)*

In the same game, San Jose defender Gabbo Gavric wins the head ball, but Kyle manages to deflect the shot off the back on a shoulder. *(Photo: Donald Echeverria)*

(Left) Kyle takes the lead in a qualifying round of the bicycle race during the 1975 Superstars competition. But this time, Kyle had to settle for third place in the over-all point total. *(Photo: United Press International)*

(Right) Kyle and teammate Ilija Mitic are ready to start an indoor game early in the 1975 season. A few weeks after this picture was taken, Mitic left Dallas to play for San Jose. *(Photo: Richard B. Lyttle)*

Kyle boots a left-footed shot during the warm-up for an indoor game. Power in both feet and good heading ability make Kyle an offensive threat in any game. *(Photo: Richard B. Lyttle)*

Typical close action of indoor soccer shows Kyle leaping in full stride as he tries to beat San Jose goaltender Mike Ivanow to the ball. San Jose won this 1975 play-off game, 8–5, and went on to take the indoor championship. *(Photo: Donald Echeverria)*

In a scramble for a high ball, Kyle's leap carries him far to the right while teammate Albert Jackson takes the header. Dallas won this 1975 game against San Jose, 1–0. *(Photo: Richard B. Lyttle)*

In the same game, Kyle has trouble with San Jose's big defender, Derek Craig, who steals the ball to block a Dallas drive. *(Photo: Richard B. Lyttle)*

Kyle heads a pass toward the goal and collides with Seattle defender Dave Gillett during hot action. *(Wide World Photo)*

steady, but they were often together, either by themselves or with other friends.

Love grew slowly for Kyle. Because of the divorce in his family, he was very cautious about the whole idea of marriage. Besides, his future seemed unclear.

After earning a degree in psychology, he hoped to enter law school. But the Army might draft him right after graduation. Also Kyle continued to think about a career in sports. He might still try for a professional contract in football, either as a kicker or a wide receiver. And then there was the possibility of pro soccer.

His performance with the Tigers was outstanding. In his second year, he scored sixteen goals in the twelve-game season, almost matching his first year's record. Then in his third year, he did match it with seventeen goals.

He undoubtedly could have made that eighteen. Kyle always took penalty kicks for the team, but in the final game of the season, he gave the honor to a teammate. He wanted to help the teammate improve his record.

Kyle, however, had to look at some hard

facts. Soccer might be big at Sewanee. The crowds were just as large for soccer games as they were for football games. But what about the outside world? The Tigers did not receive much national attention. To make things worse, the team posted a losing record in Kyle's senior year.

Kyle decided he would have a better chance with football than soccer if he wanted to become a professional athlete.

But then on the night of February 8, 1972, Kyle received a phone call from Joe Echelle in Dallas. Echelle was general manager of the Tornado.

Tomorrow, Echelle explained, the North American Soccer League would hold its college draft. And Newman wanted Kyle. Did he have other plans? Was there any reason Kyle could not sign with the club after he graduated in June?

Kyle was almost too surprised to answer. But he managed to tell Echelle that he would be glad to be drafted by the Tornado.

The next day, Dallas named Kyle as its first pick. He was delighted. He would have the chance to play professional soccer in his own hometown. And better yet, his future now was clear. He could start making plans—big plans.

Kyle and Mary Lynne were married in the Sewanee chapel the day after graduation. Then the newlyweds headed for Dallas. They found a small apartment on the north side of the city. As soon as they were settled, Kyle reported to Newman for practice.

The first practice session jolted Kyle. He found that the professional game differed vastly from college soccer. He had much to learn. He would have to work very hard if he ever hoped to make the Tornado's starting line-up.

But the worst part of that first session came in the locker room after the final scrimmage. Kyle was in the shower, where he could hear his new teammates talking about him in the next room.

All agreed that Kyle looked terrible during practice. Most predicted that he would never make the grade. Goalie Ken Cooper was the only one who stood up for Kyle. Cooper said he thought the newcomer had the right attitude.

"It takes talent, too," someone said.

"Yeah, chum, attitude alone doesn't do it," said another.

"All right, lads," Cooper said. "I'll bet a week's salary that Rote makes it."

Kyle listened to find out how many would take the bet. Surprisingly, no one did, but he still felt miserable.

How could he justify Cooper's faith in him? Somehow, Kyle vowed, he would find a way. It meant starting over. He may have been a college star, but now he would have to swallow his pride and admit he was just a beginner in a new game. And beginners weren't ashamed to ask for help.

In the days that followed, Kyle talked to his teammates. He told each one that any help would be received gladly. He said he really believed he could learn if everyone was willing to help him.

It worked. After almost every practice, one player would stay on the field with Kyle and work with him to develop an individual skill.

John Best, a defender with eighteen years of experience in the pro game, helped Kyle improve his heading technique. Defenders Dick Hall and Jim Benedek showed Kyle how to outsmart a defensive backfield, how to find open space, how to maneuver to the best shooting positions.

Midfielder Bob Ridley coached the newcomer in kicks that always meant trouble for goalies. They were shots that dropped suddenly or hit the turf with a skid.

Brazilian Luiz Juracy, a forward who had played against the great Pelé, told Kyle he must always move with controlled muscle tension. Then he would be able to change direction quickly and take advantage of all offensive opportunities.

Cooper, backing Kyle from the start, revealed some trade secrets. The All-League goalie told Kyle exactly which offensive moves and which shots a goalie feared the most.

Kyle had joined the club when the 1972 season was almost half over, and he did not make the line-up that season. No one had expected him to, but his progress surprised everyone.

Kyle learned quickly, and his willingness to work long hours was really impressive. Well before the season came to an end, every member of the team was pulling for him.

Team practices were usually held four days a week. Kyle worked out seven days a week. When the season came to a close, he continued on the same schedule.

He kept to his daily workout after he started classes at Southern Methodist University, where he planned to earn a law degree. He was busy, and so was Mary Lynne. She had taken an office job to beef up the family income.

The Rotes also taught Sunday school and were always willing to help out with other functions at their church. And Kyle soon began doing promotion work for the Tornado front office. He was well known in the Dallas area, and he had that famous name. It helped boost fan interest in soccer.

Though his schedule seemed to grow busier and busier, Kyle rarely missed his daily workout. Staying in shape helped his confidence. He knew he would need plenty of confidence for the coming season.

But when preseason training began early in 1973, Ron Newman had no thought of putting Kyle in the starting line-up.

No one could deny that Kyle had improved.

It was really amazing how his hard work was paying off. Even if improvement continued, however, the coach thought Kyle would be best used as a substitute in 1973.

But as Newman watched Kyle in scrimmages and exhibition games, the coach changed his mind. He realized that Kyle had to be the center forward in his starting line-up when the season opened. Newman had no other choice.

The coach announced his decision to start Kyle just a few days before the opener with the Toronto Metros. Kyle was thrilled. And so were his fans. Nothing, not even a torrential rain, would keep them from seeing Kyle Rote, Jr., in his first professional soccer match. And what a match it turned out to be—with Kyle racing over the wet carpet at Texas Stadium to post a goal and an assist.

CHAPTER 7
ROOKIE YEAR

Midway through the season, before the start of an important game, Newman benched Kyle. Kyle could not understand it. The St. Louis Stars might be tough, but even as Kyle watched play begin, he thought he saw ways to get around their defense.

Kyle just couldn't understand it.

After his spectacular performance in that opening game, Kyle had gone on playing well. And the team had a fine record.

Yes, there had been a couple of losses, and they were followed by a couple of shaky wins. But then the Dallas players began working together like a well-oiled machine.

Actually, St. Louis was the only team now threatening Dallas's division lead. So this was indeed an important game. But here Kyle was on the bench. Why?

Newman said Kyle had been trying too hard. He had grown fearful of making mistakes. He had lost his confidence. Kyle didn't agree with that one bit. But you can't argue with the coach.

Newman, after all, was usually right. The coach had taken over the club in 1968 after a twenty-one-game losing streak.

At that time, the Dallas Tornado looked like millionaire Lamar Hunt's biggest mistake in sports franchise ownership.

But Newman turned things around, and in 1971 he guided the team to the NASL championship. The following year, the Tornado made it to the semifinals, and this year it seemed certain that the team would be in the playoffs again.

But first, Dallas had to take care of St. Louis. And at the moment, the two teams were deadlocked in a scoreless tie. Kyle began glancing at the clock. The vital minutes ticked away. The deadlock continued well into the second half.

A loss to St. Louis would break a winning streak for Dallas. And that, Kyle feared, might sink his team's spirit at a crucial time in the season. Kyle looked at the clock again. He could hardly sit still.

Finally, the Dallas offense took fire. Bob Ridley broke into the open in front of the St. Louis goal. He took a quick crossing pass and kicked a hard shot.

The ball was blocked. So was Ridley. He fell down and rolled over, clutching a twisted knee. He would have to leave the game.

Newman looked at the bench and signaled for Kyle. Kyle sprinted onto the field, pointing at the clock, and shouting to his teammates. Just twenty minutes remained in the game.

For six minutes, Kyle helped his team press a strong offense. The ball went back and forth across the St. Louis goal. Finally a high crossing pass came in for Rick Reynolds, Kyle's partner on the forward line. But before Reynolds could reach it, a St. Louis defender jumped to head the ball away. It was a bad play. Instead of clearing the ball, the defender knocked it down just fourteen yards from the goal.

Kyle was there to blast it into the net.

It happened so fast that even Kyle's teammates were surprised. But it did not take St. Louis long to launch a counterattack. One of the Stars' offensives faltered with an offside call. Another ended with a spectacular Cooper save.

The Stars grew desperate. They gambled with an all-out offense. And they lost the gamble.

With few defenders in the Stars' backfield, Kyle got the ball. He passed off to midfielder Ilija Mitic to start a fast give-and-go play. Mitic and Kyle raced toward the St. Louis goal, sending the ball back and forth between them in a quick series of short passes.

Soon Kyle had position for a shot. The ball came to him. He hesitated, drawing the last defender out. Then Kyle passed back to Mitic. Mitic was wide open. He slammed the ball into the net.

Dallas took the game, 2–0. In just twenty minutes, Kyle added another goal and another assist to his record.

Newman decided that Kyle would be in the starting line-up for the rest of the season.

The Tornado went on to win its division title and make the playoffs for the third year in a row. Moreover, the club collected more total points for the season than any other club in the league. This meant that all of the Tornado's playoff games would be at home.

But it was Kyle's individual record that the fans followed with the most interest and suspense.

Going into the season's closer against the New York Cosmos, Kyle had nine goals and ten assists. The NASL's point system gave two points for a goal and one point for an assist. This meant that Kyle had twenty-eight points for the season. He was just one point behind the Miami Toros' Warren Archibald in the competition for the league's scoring title.

Could he win the title in the final game? Kyle's teammates wanted to make sure he did.

The Tornado lost the game to New York, 4–3, but it didn't change the team standings. The loss wasn't too important. What was important happened in the closing minutes. Dallas was awarded a penalty kick.

Ilija Mitic was the team's sharpshooter. He usually took the set shots twelve yards out from the opponent's goal. But as soon as the penalty was called against New York for roughness in the penalty box, Mitic pointed to Kyle.

"You take it," Mitic said, backing off.

Kyle nodded, swallowed, and tried to catch his breath. He eyed the ball, deciding where he wanted to put it. Then he took his run and blasted it.

Goal! Two points for Kyle. He was the NASL scoring champ for 1973! His teammates rushed him and lifted him off the ground.

What a way to end the season! But it wasn't over. Just a few days after that final game, league officials named the Rookie of the Year.

It was Kyle Rote, Jr.

Kyle could hardly believe it. Bob Rigby, the Philadelphia Atoms' outstanding goalie, and Joe Fink, the Cosmos' talented forward, had been strong contenders for top rookie honors. Beating out those two was really something.

Kyle felt very proud.

Now, if Dallas could just take the NASL crown, it would be a perfect season.

The team got off to a good start in the championship battle by beating the Cosmos in a tight semifinal game. There was only one goal scored. It came in the eighteenth minute of play when Mike Renshaw kicked a perfect pass to Kyle just ten feet away from the Cosmos' goal. Kyle slammed the ball in.

The rest of the day belonged to Ken Cooper. He saved shot after shot by the Cosmos' offense to preserve the lead right up to the final whistle.

So it was on to the Super Bowl in Dallas, where the Tornado would face the Philadelphia Atoms.

For an expansion team, the Atoms had turned in a remarkably good year. Of course, the Dallas fans liked to call it a lucky year. And certainly, luck could not carry them to the championship.

But the Dallas players took the Atoms seriously. They were good. And when the whole season came down to ninety minutes of soccer, you had to expect a hard, rough-and-tumble game.

The pressure on Kyle was terrific. As scoring ace and as the league's top rookie, he knew that everyone in the stadium would be looking for him to lead his team to victory.

It was not to be.

The Atoms' coach, Al Miller, assigned fullback Chris Dunleavy from England to guard Kyle. Miller told Dunleavy not to give Kyle any breathing room, to try to keep the rookie off balance.

If anyone could do the job, it was Dunleavy. He could run hard. He was strong. And he was tough.

Kyle was bumped, blocked, and shoved. He rarely got his foot on the ball. The fans booed. They thought the referee was letting Dunleavy get away with murder.

Kyle thought so too. On one important play when Kyle and Dunleavy went up for a headball, Kyle was shoved so that both players missed the ball. Kyle thought a foul would certainly be called this time. In fact, he turned away from the play, expecting a whistle.

But no whistle sounded. And the ball was scooting toward the Dallas goal. John Best made a desperate attempt to clear it, but he only managed to deflect it into his own net, beyond the reach of a lunging Cooper. Dallas had scored the first goal against itself.

It was hard to get back into the game after that. Kyle never was able to shake Dunleavy, and in the closing minutes of play, the Atoms scored again. They took the game, 2–0, and went home with the championship trophy.

It was a disappointing finish for the Dallas players. But they did not have to be ashamed of their record or their play. And thanks to Kyle, they had helped achieve a great advance for a game they loved.

Kyle had shown that an American-born athlete could play soccer with the best of them. Now it really looked as if soccer could become an American game.

CHAPTER 8
"SUPERSTARS"

In February the days dawn cold in Florida. It was thirty-two degrees—freezing—when Kyle walked onto the tennis court to face O. J. Simpson.

A football star playing tennis against a soccer star? Yes. This was the television program "Superstars 1974." And Kyle and "The Juice" were to compete in the first of eight events held to determine the best athlete of the year.

Simpson took a quick lead. Kyle tried to forget the sharp cold and think about nothing but the game. It would be over in just one set.

Simpson had already stretched his lead in

games to 4–2. And he had Kyle 30–15 in the next game. But then Kyle changed tactics.

He had been trying to trade hard shots with Simpson, but "The Juice" was too quick, strong, and accurate to be overpowered by the hard game. Kyle began lobbing the ball.

The change surprised and unsettled Simpson. And after a few lobs, Kyle found that he could hit the hard shot from time to time and catch his opponent off guard.

Kyle won four games in a row and took the game and the match, 6–4.

It was a fine comeback. Kyle could be pleased. But he was still in a daze.

Six months ago, the chance just to meet O. J. Simpson was nothing but a dream for Kyle. But here he had played tennis with him. And today and tomorrow, Kyle would compete against some of the other great men in sports —Pete Rose of baseball, Dick Anderson and Franco Harris of football, John Havlicek and Jim McMillian of basketball, Stan Smith of tennis; Brian Oldfield, the shot-putter; and Bob Seagren, the pole vaulter.

It really was all like a dream.

The dream started to come true soon after

the 1973 soccer season ended. Kyle learned that he was among the twenty-four athletes invited to Rotonda, Florida, to compete.

The news came when Kyle had just made a big change in plans. He had given up his law studies and had enrolled in the Perkins School of Theology. Instead of becoming a lawyer, he would go into the ministry.

The theology classes were new and difficult for Kyle, but he knew he must find time for a heavy training schedule to prepare for "Superstars." It was the chance of a lifetime.

The program was sponsored by ABC Television. That meant national television coverage. It meant top publicity. Kyle needed publicity desperately.

He did not want it for himself. He wanted it for soccer. To help soccer as much as possible, he knew that he must do more than just please his fans. He also must find new fans for the game.

His outstanding rookie year had not really won new fans. Unfortunately, most of the public still thought of Kyle as the son of a famous football player. If Kyle was to help soccer become a major sport, he would have to find national fame on his own. A good showing in the "Superstars" competition could do it.

Kyle picked his events and trained for hours each day.

At the time he received his invitation to Florida, Kyle did not own a tennis racket or a bicycle. But he picked tennis and bike racing as two of his events.

His golf clubs were a starter set given to him by his parents when he was twelve years old. But he signed up for golf in "Superstars." He would also compete in baseball hitting, swimming, bowling, the half-mile run, and the obstacle course.

Kyle's friends helped him train. Local tennis clubs, golf courses, and bowling-alley owners opened their doors for him. And Kyle often worked out with his old friend Henry Davis.

Meanwhile, Kyle and Mary Lynne bought bicycles and used them for almost all their short trips and errands.

Under "Superstars" rules, a player could not compete in his specialty. Stan Smith could not play tennis. Pete Rose could not enter the baseball-hitting contest. But there was no event using soccer skills. Actually, Kyle had always been a good swimmer. He thought that would be his best event. But his first workout in the Dallas YMCA pool gave him a shock. He could hardly swim ten strokes without running out of breath. He had to train as hard for swimming as for all the other events.

His first test came in the elimination rounds of competition. Kyle had no trouble at all. He finished first in his group, over such athletes as tennis ace Rod Laver, slugger Reggie Jackson, and pitcher Jim Palmer.

So now Kyle and eleven others were in a battle for points in the finals. A first in any event was worth 10 points. A second was worth 7 points; a third, 4 points; a fourth, 2 points; and a fifth, 1 point.

But beating O. J. Simpson in tennis earned Kyle nothing more than the right to go against Boston Celtic star John Havlicek in the second round of play. Again, Kyle fell behind. But once more he made a comeback and took a 6–3 win.

One more match remained—the finals between Kyle and Jim McMillian of the Buffalo Braves. It was another close game, but Kyle took an early lead this time and held it to win the match, 6–4, and take first place in the tennis competition. Ten points for Kyle.

From the tennis courts, he went immediately to the golf links for 9 holes of play. Dick Anderson shot a 41 to win, but Kyle had a fine round. He shot a 43 for second place and 7 more points.

Swimming came next on the busy, first-day schedule. Kyle went out to swim 100 meters at top speed. Bob Seagren stayed with him all the way, but Kyle reached the finish with a single-stroke lead. Another 10 points.

Kyle now had a big lead over all the other stars. The next event was bowling. Kyle expected to do well.

He did. While some of the others were complaining about the heavy pace of the day, Kyle felt fresh and confident. He bowled a 10-frame total of 214 pins, good enough for another first. Another 10 points.

Kyle ended the day with three firsts and a second, and 37 points.

Could anyone catch up in the second day? Seagren almost made it.

Kyle finished a second in the bicycle race,

close behind Austrian skier Karl Schranz. The next three events were baseball batting, the half-mile run, and the obstacle course. Kyle failed to win any points in them. Seagren had a big day, but he couldn't catch up with Kyle. Seagren's total two-day record gave him 38 points. Kyle had 44.

Kyle Rote, Jr., thus became the top athlete of the "Superstars 1974" competition.

He was given a big trophy and a check for $54,000. The winnings were based on his point total in the eliminations and the finals.

Kyle and Mary Lynne had never seen that much money. And, of course, reporters wanted to know how they would spend it.

Some of it, Kyle said, would be given away. They always gave a tenth of all their earnings to their church. There was no reason to stop doing that now.

Actually, Kyle knew that the publicity from his "Superstars" win was worth millions to soccer. A national television audience was getting its first close look at an American soccer player. And Kyle made the most of it.

The television audience had to like what it saw. Here was a friendly athlete signing autographs, talking to children, smiling at the camera, and answering questions thoughtfully and politely. Here was a likable, modest, and sincere young man. A real winner. Everybody's superstar. And he happened to be a soccer player.

Yes, Kyle's victory was worth millions.

But it was very strange. The prize money—$54,000—was thirty-eight times Kyle's annual salary from the Tornado. He was not being paid what he was worth.

Phil Woosnam (left), commissioner of the North American Soccer League, talks to Pelé and Kyle during a 1975 press conference held in Pelé's honor at San Jose. *(Photo: Richard B. Lyttle)*

Kyle and Pelé team up for a half-time talk before the television camera at the 1975 championship game. Tampa Bay won the game by beating Portland, 2–0. *(Photo: Richard B. Lyttle)*

In a 1976 preseason game, Kyle outjumps two San Jose defenders and the goaltender to win this head ball, but he failed to score. This game ended in a 0–0 tie. *(Photo: Donald Echeverria)*

Kyle goes high for a header, trying to set up a shot for a teammate in front of the San Jose goal. Dallas, however, failed to score, and San Jose won this 1976 match, 4-0. *(Photo: Donald Echeverria)*

In the same game, San Jose's John Rowlands, with an arm linked around Kyle's wrist, heads the ball (even with the top of the grandstand) away from the San Jose goal. *(Photo: Donald Echeverria)*

Kyle and San Jose goaltender Mike Hewitt collide in the air as both try to reach the ball during a 1976 play-off game. Dallas lost the game, 2–0, and lost its hope for the championship. *(Photo: Donald Echeverria)*

In the same game, Kyle leaps to head the ball above defender Buzz Demling during a Dallas attack. *(Photo: Donald Echeverria)*

Kyle waits until the last minute to draw defender Laurie Calloway to the ball. Then Kyle passes to a teammate. The tactics are good, but Dallas was not good enough to advance in the 1976 play-off bid at San Jose. *(Photo: Donald Echeverria)*

Kyle and other stars of the NASL wear Tampa Bay Rowdies jerseys for the 1977 exhibition game with touring stars from the People's Republic of China. China won the game, 2–1. *(Photo: United Press International)*

CHAPTER 9
ON THE RUN

Before the 1974 soccer season came to a close, some Dallas sportswriters began to criticize Kyle. And more than a few fans were angry with him.

Sports has always been a crazy business. It was crazy to criticize someone who had already done as much as Kyle. It was crazy to be angry with someone who kept trying as hard as he did.

But Kyle understood. And there were moments when he was angry with himself.

Take that midseason game in Los Angeles. At halftime, the Tornado led the Aztecs, 2–0, but in the second half, the Dallas players let down. Los Angeles tied the score and forced postgame penalty shots. Under the league's new tie-breaker system, each side took a series of five penalty kicks. The win went to the team scoring more in the series.

Kyle's shot missed and Dallas lost the game.

Kyle felt terrible. Soon afterward, Newman benched him.

The fans, of course, expected Kyle to repeat the outstanding performance of his rookie year. Actually, Kyle had a good second year, but it was not as good as his first. The fans felt let down.

And there was another thing. The typical sports fan resents players who ask for more money. Right after his "Superstars 1974" win, Kyle had asked for and received a big raise.

The year before, Kyle had been paid just $1,400 for the whole season. Now he was earning $15,000. Even this was small compared with the pay in other professional sports, but it was a living wage. Kyle had insisted on that.

For too long, the pay in soccer had been very low. Few players in the league received more than $3,000 for a season. Most of them had to hold down other jobs just to pay for the necessities of life. As long as the low pay continued, Kyle believed, soccer would remain a minor sport. Fans would not take the game seriously. Promising soccer players would go into other sports.

The "Superstars 1974" win gave Kyle the chance to change this. He called public attention to the low pay. And by winning his own raise, he took the first step in raising the pay for everyone.

Of course, it brought fan criticism. But players throughout the league loved Kyle for what he had done.

One criticism of Kyle may have been justified: He tried to do too much off the playing field. After the "Superstars 1974" win, it seemed that everyone wanted him to make public appearances, give speeches, and sit for interviews.

Kyle did not know how to turn people down. No meeting, whether it was a dinner club or a church group, was ever too small. He seemed to be on the run constantly.

Actually, there were many big events where Kyle's appearances helped promote soccer. In

June, for instance, he and basketball star Rick Barry teamed up to win a doubles tennis tournament for celebrities at Las Vegas, Nevada. The tournament was well covered by newspapers and television.

Later in the season, Kyle made a quick trip to London, England, to attend a banquet and present an award to English soccer's Rookie of the Year.

Meanwhile, Kyle's promotion work in the Tornado front office took more and more of his time.

But Kyle never neglected his training. He always worked hard in practice. And he played hard. Still, he did not always play up to his own standards.

He faced one obvious problem. Several changes had been made on the team. The Dallas defense was not as good as it had been the year before. Kyle had to run back again and again to help out on defense. All the running left him exhausted at the end of a game.

Another problem was not so obvious. Kyle did not discover it until the season was half over. But he finally had to admit that he was too ambitious. He had been trying to do things that he did not have the skill to do.

For instance, he thought he could help the offense if he attacked from the wing. But he did not have the skill to be effective from outside. He was much better up the center. Each time he left the center, he hurt himself and his team.

Unfortunately, he discovered his mistake about the time Newman benched him. And at that point, the criticism of Kyle reached its peak.

Actually, criticism did not bother him greatly. He knew it was part of his job. If it did anything, criticism just made him work harder.

And he did work hard. Watching a game from the bench was a tough experience. He had to be ready at any moment to go in as a substitute. It was easier and much more fun to be in for the entire game. Kyle went all out in practice, and it did not take him long to earn back his position as a starter.

As it worked out, Kyle missed only two full games in the 1974 season. And he had a good record—seven goals and two assists for a total of sixteen points to become leading scorer of his team. Better yet, the Tornado finished first in its division and went into the NASL playoffs for the fourth year in a row.

The Miami Toros knocked Dallas out in the semifinals, 3–0. Then Los Angeles beat the Toros, 4–3, to take the league championship.

But still, it had not been a bad year for Kyle. Despite some of the criticism, he felt he had learned a great deal. He now knew some of the difficulties of being a substitute. And he knew how to adjust his game.

He also realized that he would have to adjust his life. His public appearances and his promotion work left him little time to be at home. Also, his mother had been seriously ill, and Kyle had been able to spend very little time with her.

Then, soon after the season ended, Kyle was picked for the United States national team. It was a great honor. He would represent his country in international matches. He might even help the team make it into World Cup competition.

But the national team would make further demands on his time. He had to do something.

He and Mary Lynne had a long talk. They decided that Kyle would have to drop out of theology school. He still wanted to become a minister, but he could return to school later, when he had more time.

Meanwhile, he could use his position in sports as the "pulpit" for his beliefs. He could go on talking to church groups about his faith and his values.

Without the pressure of homework and classes, Kyle was able to find time for another important job. He began preparing to defend his "Superstars" title. The competition was scheduled for early in 1975.

As usual, he trained very hard. Once again, he made it to the finals easily.

But this year, the competition was tougher. O. J. Simpson and Bob Seagren had both come back determined to take the title.

But Kyle again won a comeback match from Simpson in tennis. And once again, he beat Seagren in swimming. The bowling, however, was a disappointment. Kyle got a fourth there. He finished the first day with 22 points.

He would have to score high in the second day to retain his title. But the best he could do was third in the bicycle race, fourth in the half-mile run and in baseball hitting, and fifth in the obstacle course.

Simpson won "Superstars 1975" with 47½ points. Seagren was second, with 40 points. Kyle, with 31 points, took third.

Sure, Kyle was sorry not to win, but he had tried as hard as he could, and he had forced two men to give their very best to beat him.

Besides, Simpson and Seagren would be around for some time. Kyle would have a crack at them again next year. And maybe next year, things would ease up for him so he could have a little more time to get ready.

CHAPTER 10
WASHED UP?

The television cameras were all pointed at the players' entrance tunnel. Sports photographers lined both sides of a pathway to the field. And 21,278 fans sat ready to make New York's Downing Stadium erupt.

The national television crews, the photographers, and the excited fans were watching for the first appearance of Edson Arantes do Nascimento in a New York Cosmos uniform.

Yes, Pelé had come to America.

The great Brazilian forward, the best-known athlete in the world, wanted to help the growth of soccer in the United States. He could do it. During his career, warring nations had declared peace to see him play. His own country had declared him a national asset.

Now Pelé had just signed a three-year contract with the Cosmos for $4.7 million. He was worth every cent of it.

Although his playing days were coming to a close, he was still one of the most skillful men in soccer. His instinct for the game never failed. And he possessed an electric personality.

When he ran onto the field and waved, the New York crowd went wild. And when Pelé smiled—pandemonium!

It was June 15, 1975. Pelé's first NASL game would be an exhibition match—the Cosmos against the Dallas Tornado.

Yes, Kyle was there. He was just as thrilled as any of the fans. Playing on the same field with Pelé was another dream come true.

And the game turned into something to remember. Surprisingly, Dallas pounded out a 2–0 lead in the first half. What happened to Pelé? Remember, he was playing for the first time with new teammates. He needed a little time to find out what they could do, a little time to organize his offense.

It did not take long. In the second half, Pelé led the Cosmos in a series of stunning attacks. The Dallas defense worked hard, but it could not stop Pelé. He scored one goal and assisted on another before the final whistle blew.

So it ended in a tie, 2–2. The Cosmos' comeback put a fine finish to a great day in the history of soccer.

The reporters, of course, crowded around Pelé for postgame interviews. It seemed that they wanted to know his views on everything and everybody in America. Someone asked what he thought of Kyle.

"He has the potential to be a world-class player," Pelé said. "He reads the game well."

Later, Kyle was asked how he felt after playing against Pelé. "Today," Kyle said with a happy grin, "our sport emerged from minor-league status."

Naturally, Kyle felt honored and very proud to have been on the field with Pelé. And, although he did not say so at the time, Kyle also felt relieved.

After Kyle's great rookie year, the league had looked on him as the big drawing card.

And since the league and the fans expected great things from him, he played under pressure all the time. Kyle didn't mind, but after the "Superstars 1974" win, the pressure increased tremendously.

As the best-known man in American soccer, he was expected to perform miracles. He had been playing a very difficult role. Now, thank goodness, it was over.

Pelé would now play the lead role. He would take the pressure. He would be the game's top promoter. He would be the man the league looked to for big publicity stories and big gates at games.

As it worked out, Pelé did all that was expected of him. Before his three-year contract ended, he drew a crowd that set a North American record for attendance—77,691 fans at a single game.

Kyle would continue making public appearances, giving speeches, playing in celebrity tennis matches, and helping his club with the promotion work.

But the pressure was off. And best of all, it looked as if he might find a little more free time to be with friends and family than he had in the past.

It didn't happen. Kyle was just as busy off the field in 1975 as he had ever been.

Early in the year, he attended a banquet where the Dallas Chamber of Commerce honored him with the "Big D" award, an award given each year to the person who had done the most to bring national attention to the city of Dallas.

Soon after that, Tornado management named Kyle director of development and put him in charge of soccer camps run for the youth of the Dallas-Fort Worth area. More hard work? You bet.

And on the field, Kyle found himself playing another role. He had become unofficial leader of the team.

Even older players who were more experienced than Kyle respected his opinions. Kyle was not afraid to speak out about problems on the team or in the league.

He was among the first to say that the players needed a union, and he made no bones about his views on indoor soccer.

The league started indoor matches early in

1975 as an experiment. At first, most players welcomed the idea because it meant a longer season and more pay.

But there was a problem. Kyle recognized it right away. The indoor game was played in an arena the same size as a hockey rink. With little space to maneuver, the players were bound to bump into each other. The bumps led to rough play.

Referees could not prevent the roughness. Some fine players missed the entire outdoor season because of broken legs or arms suffered during an indoor match. Kyle had been right. After two years, the league dropped indoor soccer to optional play for individual clubs. The experiment had not worked.

Fortunately, Kyle escaped injury and he carved out another fine record in the 1975 outdoor season. His five goals and six assists gave him another 16 points. Once again, he was his team's leading scorer.

But the team itself did not have a good year.

With just nine wins against thirteen losses, Dallas finished fourth in its division. The team failed to make it to the playoffs for the first time in four years.

Poor years bring changes.

Newman was fired and replaced by Al Miller, former coach of the Philadelphia Atoms. Dick Berg was brought in from the San Jose Earthquakes as the new general manager. The club found a new playing field, moving from Texas Stadium to Ownby Stadium on the Southern Methodist University campus.

Even the uniforms changed. White jerseys with blue-and-white trim replaced the old red-and-white jerseys.

All the changes stirred up the club. Everyone expected great things in 1976.

For Kyle, the year opened with a bang. He went back to Florida and won the "Superstars" title again. He did it by edging out Lynn Swann of the Pittsburgh Steelers by 4 points, 33–29.

Under the rules, Kyle couldn't compete again in the future. Someday, another athlete may match his feat by winning the title twice in three years, but Kyle will always be remembered as the man who did it first.

The year 1976 was a good one for the Tornado. The team won thirteen and lost eleven for the season, good enough for second place in its division and another shot at the NASL championship.

But the San Jose Earthquakes put Dallas out in the second round of postseason play. Dallas seemed to be jinxed in the playoffs. The Toronto Metros went on to take the league crown.

Just the same, it had been a good season for Dallas. Kyle, however, hit rough times in 1976. His scoring totals dropped to three goals and three assists for just nine points. And he spent more time on the bench than ever before. Although he appeared in nineteen games, he had just six full games to his credit.

Was he to spend the rest of his soccer career as a substitute? You might think so if you listened to his critics. One writer said that play around the league had improved 80 per cent since Kyle's rookie year, but that Kyle had improved just 10 per cent. In short, the writer said, Kyle was washed up.

Could it be true?

Why not let the record for 1977 speak for itself? No one worked harder than Kyle in preseason training. He was determined to return to the starting line-up. And he did. He played in every one of the 1977 season's twenty-four games. And he produced.

He scored eleven goals and six assists, earning a total of twenty-eight points. The total not only made him his team's leading scorer once again, but it also put him in sixth place overall in league scoring totals. And of the five players scoring more points than he, none was an American-born player.

Meanwhile, thanks to Kyle, the Tornado nailed down the best record in team history—seventeen wins and only seven losses. It was a powerhouse team, one of the best in the league.

But once again, the Tornado lost out in the playoffs, falling this time to Los Angeles in first-round action. This year, the championship finally went to the New York Cosmos.

The next year, 1978, Kyle's sixth full season with Dallas, brought some disappointments and a big surprise. Though still a starter, Kyle was often replaced before games ended. And the club's record of fourteen wins against sixteen losses was not good enough for a spot in the play-offs. The Cosmos again took the Super Bowl to become the league's first two-time champions.

Kyle had performed well, well enough to win a spot on the league's All North American All-Star Team, and he believed he could make another strong contribution to the Tornado next season. But then came the big surprise.

Dallas sold Kyle to the Houston Hurricane, a team that had just struggled through its first year with poor attendance and a miserable, ten-twenty win-loss record.

Kyle was jolted. He had hoped to finish his playing career with Dallas. The club management explained that Houston had made an offer that was simply too good to turn down—half a million in cash for Kyle's three-year contract.

Then Hurricane general manager Hans von Mende told the press that Kyle was just what the new club needed to cure its problems both on the field and at the gate.

"We feel, with the acquisition of Kyle, we have made a commitment to have a quality product," Von Mende said. "He's an inspiration—"

After these words, the deal began to look

good. Kyle realized that he faced a new and exciting challenge, a real chance to increase his contribution to soccer.

Will he meet the challenge? You can be sure that he will give it his very best. He always does. He always makes things happen.

In the years to come, these things can be certain. The Houston Hurricane will be the team, and Kyle Rote, Jr.—everyone's superstar—will be the man to watch in American soccer.

INDEX

ABC television, *see* "Superstars 1974"; "Superstars 1975"; "Superstars 1976"
Anderson, Dick, 58, 62
Archibald, Warren, 52

Barry, Rick, 68
Baseball in "Superstars" competitions, 60, 63, 72
Benedek, Jim, 44
Berg, Dick, 79
Best, John, 9, 44, 55
Bicycle racing in "Superstars" competitions, 60, 62–63
Black Bandits (team), 19–21, 33–35
Blackpool (England), 20
Bowling in "Superstars" competitions, 60, 62, 71

Chinese Bandits (team), 19
College Athletic Conference, 36

Collins, John, 8
Cooper, Ken, 43–44, 51, 54, 56

Dallas (Tex.)
  Chamber of Commerce, 77
  Kyle's birth in, 11
  Kyle's boyhood in, 15–23
  Kyle's later home in, 43
Dallas Cowboys, 35
Dallas Tornado
  coaches of, 79
  Kyle with, 42–82
    drafted, 42–43
    1973 season, 1–10, 47–56
    1974 season, 65–70
    1975 season, 74–79
    1976 season, 80
    1977 season, 80–81
    1978 season, 81–82
    practice sessions, 43–47, 68
    promotional work, 46, 68, 70, 76, 77

salary, 64, 66–67
scouted, 33–35
sold, 82
unionizing, 77
uniforms of, 79
Davis, Henry, 16, 18, 24, 29–30, 37, 60
Delta Tau Delta fraternity, 38
Dunleavy, Chris, 55–56

Echelle, Joe, 42
England, Kyle's trips to, 21–22, 68

Fink, Joe, 53

Golf in "Superstars" competitions, 60, 62
Green Bay Packers, 13
Griffith, Ron, 20–22

Hall, Dick, 44
Harris, Franco, 58
Havlicek, John, 58, 61
Highland Park High School (Dallas, Tex.), 16–18, 22–23, 24
Houston Hurricane, Kyle sold to, 82–83
Hunt, Lamar, 49

Indoor soccer, 77–78

Jackson, Reggie, 61
Juracy, Luiz, 45

Las Vegas (Nev.), 68
Laver, Rod, 61
Lombardi, Vince, 13–14
Longhorn Soccer Club, 21

Los Angeles Aztecs, 81
1974 games of, 65–66, 70
Louisiana State University, 19

McMillian, Jim, 58, 61
Miami Toros, 52, 70
Miller, Al, 55, 79
Mitic, Ilija, 51, 53

Newman, Ron
coaching ability of, 49
fired, 79
1973 season, 50, 52
puts Kyle in starting lineup, 2–3, 47, 52
1974 season, 66, 69
scouts Kyle, 33–35
New Rochelle (N.Y.), Kyle's boyhood in, 12–15
New York City, Kyle's boyhood in, 11–12
New York Cosmos, 81, 82
1973 games of, 52–54
Pelé with, 73–76
New York Giants (football team), Kyle's father with, 12–15
North American Soccer League (NASL)
college draft of, 42
1973 scoring champ of, 52–53
1978 All North American All-Star Team, 82

Oklahoma State University (OSU), Kyle at, 24, 26–32, 35
Oldfield, Brian, 58

85

Order of Gownsmen
    (Sewanee), 38
Ownby Stadium, Dallas moves
    to, 79

Palmer, Jim, 61
Pelé, 45, 73–76
Peyser, Dr. Charles, 37
Philadelphia Atoms, 53, 79
    1973 championship game,
        54–56
Players' union, 77

Renshaw, Mike, 5–6, 54
Reynolds, Rick, 50
Ridley, Bob, 45, 50
Rigby, Bob, 53
Rose, Pete, 58, 60
Rote, Betty (mother), 12, 15,
    70
Rote, Chris (brother), 12
Rote, Elizabeth (sister), 12
Rote, Gary (brother), 12
Rote, Kyle, Jr.
    accused of theft at OSU,
        30–32
    as amateur soccer player,
        18–22
    at Sewanee, 35–36, 38,
        41–42
    in auto accident, 30
    birth of, 11
    boyhood of, 11–23
    courtship and marriage of,
        40–41, 43
    as football player, 16, 18,
        22–24, 42
    injury, 26–30
    law studies of, 46, 59
    as professional soccer player
        on Houston Hurricane,
            82–83
        on U.S. national team, 70
        See also Dallas Tornado,
            Kyle with
    public appearances of, 67–68,
        70, 76
    religion and, 59, 63, 71
    in "Superstars 1974," 57–64,
        66–67, 76
    in "Superstars 1975," 71–72
    in "Superstars 1976," 79
Rote, Kyle, Sr. (father), 12–15
Rote, Mary Lynne Lykins
    (wife), 40–41, 43, 46,
    60, 63, 71
Rotonda (Fla.), 59

St. Louis Stars, 1973 game of,
    48–51
San Jose Earthquakes, 79, 80
Schranz, Karl, 63
Seagren, Bob (pole vaulter), 58,
    62, 63, 71–72
Sewanee (Tenn.), see
    University of the South
Sewanee Purple (publication),
    38
Sigler, Dr. E. A., 24, 29
Simpson, O. J., in "Superstars"
    competitions, 57–58, 61,
    71–72
Smith, Stan, 58, 60
Southern Methodist University
    (Dallas, Tex.), 12, 15,
    23, 46
    Dallas Tornado moves to
        stadium of, 79
Stillwater, see Oklahoma State
    University

Super Bowl, 82
   1973 championship game in, 54–56
"Superstars 1974" (TV program), 57–64, 66–67, 76
"Superstars 1975" (TV program), 71–72
"Superstars 1976" (TV program), 79
Swann, Lynn, 79
Swimming in "Superstars" competitions, 60–62, 71

Tennis in "Superstars" competitions, 57–59, 61–62, 71
Texas Stadium
   Dallas Tornado moves from, 79
   Dallas Tornado vs. Toronto in, 1–10, 47
Thieves at Oklahoma State University, 30–32

Tigers (team), 36–37, 41–42
Toronto Metros, 80
   1973 game of, 1–10, 47
Track
   at Sewanee, 39
   in "Superstars" competitions, 60, 63, 72

United Dundee (team), 18–19, 20
University of the South, 24–25, 29, 32
   campus of, 37–38
   Kyle's courses at, 36–37
   Kyle's courtship at, 40–41, 43
   Kyle's extracurricular activities at, 38–39
   Kyle's soccer at, 35–36, 38, 41–42

Von Mende, Hans, 82

Washington Redskins, 13

EDWARD F. DOLAN, JR., and RICHARD B. LYTTLE have been close friends for ten years. Both are native Californians and each has written several books. The Signal Books mark their first efforts as co-authors.

Mr. Lyttle was raised in Ojai, served in the Navy in World War II, and attended the University of California at Berkeley. He has worked as a cowboy, farmer, newspaper reporter, and editor. He began selling stories and articles for children in the 1950s.

Mr. Dolan's boyhood was spent in Los Angeles. After serving with the 101st Airborne Division during World War II, he attended the University of San Francisco. He began writing when he was in his teens and has also been a teacher and a newspaper reporter.

The two men met while they were reporters for rival newspapers in northern California. Mr. Lyttle and his wife, Jean, live in Point Reyes Station, north of San Francisco. Mr. Dolan and his wife, Rose, live in the nearby town of Novato.